Original title:
In the Shade of Palms

Copyright © 2025 Creative Arts Management OÜ
All rights reserved.

Author: Nathaniel Blackwood
ISBN HARDBACK: 978-1-80581-575-4
ISBN PAPERBACK: 978-1-80581-102-2
ISBN EBOOK: 978-1-80581-575-4

Sanctuary of the Swaying Singles

Underneath the tall trees bright,
The singles gather, oh what a sight!
With drinks in hand and laughter loud,
They dance like leaves, feeling proud.

Some trip over roots, oh what a mess,
While others strut in their Sunday best.
A coconut falls, they all! duck!
But laughter follows, who gives a cluck?

Shelter from the Sun's Embrace

As the sun beams down, they find their spot,
Sipping iced tea, cold and hot.
One spills a drink, it splashes wide,
They laugh and chant, 'What a ride!'

A seagull swoops, it's searching for snacks,
The crowd defends with playful attacks.
They volley chips in a wacky game,
Who knew a picnic could bring such fame?

Echoes of the Palm's Gentle Lullaby

Whispers float in the breezy air,
As hammock swings toss without a care.
A snorer snores, a sunhat flies,
A chorus of giggles mixed with sighs.

Someone gets stuck in the sway of dreams,
While others plot silly sunbeam schemes.
A daring leap into the splash,
In the light of day, they make quite a splash!

Twilight in the Tropical Embrace

As dusk arrives, colors bloom bright,
Glow-in-the-dark drinks bring pure delight.
They tell tall tales of the day's fun,
With giggles mingling, all day is done.

The shadows dance, the laughter grows,
A misfit skit, where everyone glows.
Under the stars, their joy takes flight,
With silly songs that last all night.

Ephemeral Beauty in the Breeze

A dandy bee took a dive,
In a flower, he came alive.
He missed the bloom with a smack,
Landed right on a big ol' snack.

The blooms giggle in the sun,
As petals dance, oh what fun!
The breeze teases all around,
Nature's playground, joy is found.

A Tapestry of Green and Gold

In fields where gold meets the green,
A grasshopper puts on a scene.
He struts and hops like he's in charge,
With tiny moves that are quite large.

The sun above begins to glare,
While squirrels lounge without a care.
"Why rush?" they say with a grin,
It's a grand day to just begin.

Reverence in the Rustling Palms

A parrot squawks, quite the show,
Teaching all the trees to flow.
With quirky words and offbeat tones,
Even the palm fronds laugh in groans.

As breezes tickle leafy crowns,
The lizards lounge in funny towns.
"Just chill," they wink in sunny style,
And bask in warmth, mile by mile.

Harmony Under Heaven's Canopy

In a concert, frogs croak lead,
With crickets backing, just like thread.
They serenade as night unfolds,
With laughs that echo, stories told.

A sloth hangs low, in perfect pose,
His slow dance charms, as day's light doze.
'Why rush?' he yawns, 'When fun's right here?'
With every joke, he draws them near.

Basking in Nature's Whisper

Underneath the leafy spread,
Squirrels dance on limbs ahead.
They chatter, tease, and play a game,
While I just hope I'm not to blame.

The sun peeks through in cheeky rays,
Tickling my nose in silly ways.
I giggle as the shadows chase,
A lizard leaps, oh what a race!

A breeze comes in with playful glee,
It wraps around and bothers me.
It lifts my hat, a gusty thief,
Now I'm the one who's lost belief.

Among the palms, a party's near,
Crickets sing, it's music clear.
I'll join the dance, no doubt, no fear,
And hope to leave with laughter here!

A Tapestry of Shadows and Stars

Beneath the fronds, I spy a sight,
A raccoon plotting snack delight.
His eyes are wide, his paws are sly,
Can't help but laugh, or will I cry?

The stars peep out, they wink and glow,
As I trip over roots below.
Whispering trees, they seem to care,
Nudging me back to a safer lair.

A lineup of ants in perfect row,
Marching to dance, an insect show.
With popcorn crumbs for them to munch,
I cheer them on—it's quite a bunch!

At last, the moon lets out a laugh,
As I attempt my silly dance craft.
With shadows swirling, oh what fun,
In this grand party, I am the one!

Shadowed Reflections by the Tides

Beneath the trees, where laughter swells,
A crab in a tux, with tales to tell.
It dances around, with a pinch and a glare,
While seagulls cackle, without a care.

The sun throws shadows, a jigsaw delight,
And squirrels on stilts, prepare for a fight.
With every wave, the whispers grow loud,
As fish play poker, beneath a cloud.

Embraced by the Ocean's Breath

A dolphin wearing shades, strikes a pose,
While seaweed waves to us, it knows.
The tides they giggle, with bubbles that pop,
As turtles skateboarding, just won't stop.

A crab recites poetry, oh what a show,
As fish throw confetti, in an underwater glow.
With each crash of waves, a chorus of glee,
The ocean smiles wide, dancing with me.

The Silent Murmur of Leafy Guardians

Leaves gossip softly, in playful tones,
While monkeys sip juice, on silly thrones.
A parrot explains, with flair and sass,
How to swing from branches, and never fall flat.

The ground is a trampoline, bouncy and bright,
As snails make small races, with all of their might.
Laughter fills space, like candy in air,
While shadows play tricks, it's a whimsical fair.

Whispers of Breeze and Palm

The breeze tells secrets, so cheeky and light,
As kites dance around, in a colorful flight.
A worm writes a letter, sent up to the sky,
While ants hold a meeting, to argue and sigh.

With laughter like thunder, the bugs take a stand,
While beach balls are tossed, by the whimsy of sand.
In this wacky wonder, where laughter runs fast,
Every moment is sparkly, a joy unsurpassed.

Beneath Palm Leaves

Under leafy covers, we lounge with glee,
Crabs get tipsy, sipping coconut tea.
A lizard strolls by in sunglasses it seems,
Telling funny tales of wild, wobbly dreams.

The breeze carries laughter from hidden guests,
While turtles plot naps in their cozy nests.
A party of ants disco on the ground,
Shaking their groove, oh how funny it sounds!

Stories Unfold

Old coconuts whisper their secrets untold,
About a wise seagull with feathers of gold.
He claims he can dance, though it's quite hard to see,
The rhythm he's got is just plain goofy!

Squirrels tell jokes as they munch on their snacks,
While geckos compete in their comedic acts.
With every misstep, the punchlines are found,
In this silly jungle, we all gather round.

A Haven of Green Elegance

A symphony plays with the rustle of leaves,
As frogs rehearse songs, or so one believes.
The sun peeks through gaps like a playful tease,
While shadows dance briskly—the hustle's a breeze!

Here critters parade in their finest attire,
A weasel in bowtie that never will tire.
They waddle and wobble, a comical scene,
Adding charm to this place like a sweet, vivid dream.

The Cool Breath of Nature's Canopy

Breezy days pass in a cloud of delight,
As birds chirp their tunes, a comical flight.
One landed on cactus, oh what a surprise,
Spinning around, trying hard not to cry!

The chill of the shade makes all the cats yawn,
While rabbits play poker at the break of dawn.
Lost in their games, they forget about meals,
And giggles erupt at the sight of their reels!

Beneath the Veil of Fronds

Beneath leafy drapes, mischief brews strong,
As critters unite, for they all sing along.
A walrus in flip-flops, who knew there'd be such?
Dancing with snails, oh it's simply too much!

Raccoons tell tales of treasures they've found,
But it's mostly just socks, scattered around.
In this wild garden, hilarity blooms,
For laughter and joy spread like sweet summer fumes!

A Dance of Hues Beneath the Stars

Under twinkling lights we prance,
Dodging blunders, taking a chance.
With every wobble, giggles arise,
Our clumsy moves, a grand surprise.

The breeze plays music, a lively tune,
As we spin like crazy under the moon.
Sand gets lost where feet can't roam,
We laugh and shout, this feels like home.

The Cradle of Coastal Winds

A sailboat's corkscrew in a breeze,
Sailor's hat flies off with ease.
Chasing seagulls on a wild quest,
Who knew the ocean's jokes had zest?

We dance with gulls, hands in the air,
Falling over, without a care.
Salted laughs in every wave,
Here's to messes we love to crave!

Journeys in a Leafy Refuge

Riddles from trees, branches wear,
Tickling breezes, everywhere.
Lost in laughter, we leap and sway,
Nature's pranks: come join the play!

Tripping over roots, slipping on leaves,
Giggling till our sides heave.
Squirrels snicker, what a delight,
Maybe we're wrong — they might be right!

Palm Fronds and the Whisper of Waves

Palm leaves shake in the gentle air,
Whispers of jokes that nobody's there.
With coconuts rolling about, we find,
The punchline's buried, who's in our mind?

Watch the water with its silly splash,
Crabs join in with a clumsy dash.
We chuckle hard as sand gets stuck,
In our shoes, oh what luck!

The Interlude of Tropical Winds

Breezes whisper tales of glee,
As coconuts drop with wild decree.
Laughter bounces from tree to tree,
While sunburns sprout enthusiastically.

A crab scuttles by with great flair,
Dancing like it doesn't have a care.
Flip-flops lost, we stand and stare,
Who knew the beach could be so rare?

Seagulls squawk with playful pride,
Diving low, they take a ride.
Who knew they'd be our guide?
With snacks in hand, we won't slide!

A frisbee lands in someone's drink,
A joyful mess, and what a stink!
With giggles loud, we barely think,
Life's a party, don't you wink?

Enchanted Moments of Calm and Green

Leaves chatter softly, take a chance,
As lizards join in on the dance.
We sit back, give fate a glance,
Wondering if it'll lead to romance.

Swaying palms wear hats of sun,
We sip our drinks, life's lots of fun.
But bees buzz in a hilarious run,
Chasing us, and we start to run.

A picnic spread on checkered cloth,
A sandwich added to someone's broth.
We laugh at spills, that was the truth,
Nature's comedy—wow, it's uncouth!

A turtle slowly makes its way,
As though it's here to steal the day.
With each step, we laugh and sway,
Oh, how we love this wild ballet!

Beneath the Arms of Nature's Guardians

Palm trees arch like gentle foes,
Tickling our heads as laughter flows.
A squirrel drops nuts, quite a show,
As we ponder why we can't throw?

A breeze fluffs up our beachy hair,
We think it's stylish, without a care.
But little do we know, oh dear,
A bird is nesting with feathers near!

The ocean waves make a silly sound,
As crabs dig holes without a bound.
With sandy toes, we stand our ground,
Chuckling loudly at this funny mound.

Why do flip-flops vanish so fast?
It's like they relish being outclassed.
But in this place, we're well amassed,
Silly moments—a joyous blast!

The Quietude Where Shadows Play

Underneath a leafy roof,
We share jokes that defy all proof.
An iguana joins, quite aloof,
As we all sit and spin our goof.

Laughter echoes, what a scene,
As we ask, 'Have you seen the queen?'
The sun thinks it's a radiant bean,
While shadows dance, a cheeky routine.

We sip our drinks, but oh dear me,
A drink thief is a legendary spree.
With giggles loud, we start to flee,
As nature chuckles at our decree.

So here we are, in carefree bliss,
Under shadows, we cannot miss.
With each moment a chuckling kiss,
Life's sweet humor is pure happiness!

Cupped in Earth's Warm Embrace

Underneath the leafy fan,
A lizard slips, thinks he's a man.
He struts and sways, with quite the flair,
In search of snacks he's sure to share.

Sunbathers laugh, their hats askew,
While squirrels gossip, 'Is that a shoe?'
A coconut drops, and all take heed,
Nature's bounty, a funny deed.

Children chase dreams across the sand,
With sticky toes, they make their stand.
A playful breeze joins the charade,
In nature's embrace, no plans ever made.

The Stillness at Day's End

As shadows stretch and laughter fades,
A raccoon sneaks in, making charades.
With a grin, he tips over a drink,
'Is it too late? Come join me and think!'

Birds in a row sing their last tune,
While crickets prepare for the night's cartoon.
A nearby cat rolls, proud and spry,
Declaring, 'I rule both land and sky!'

Stars twinkle on, the moon's on break,
And in the hush, one silly snake.
With a wiggle and jazz, he slithers free,
Who knew nature's fun was all about me?

Nature's Lounge and the Silent Breeze

In the garden's corner, the couch is wide,
A butterfly dances, full of pride.
Whispers of flowers tease the tune,
And ants host parties under the moon.

A lazy frog plops with a splash,
While bees buzz in, a bumbling crash.
Under the sun, the laughter glows,
As everyone dozes, sweetly doze.

Here comes the breeze, with giggles and glee,
Tugging at hats, come join the spree!
Amidst the fun, one llama appears,
Chasing a butterfly, with no fears!

Palms and Petals: A Haiku of Home

Palm fronds tickle toes,
With giggles blending in laughs,
Flowers play peekaboo.

Sun does its dance here,
Breeze whispers tales untold,
Laughter fills the air.

Petals and Palms

Beneath the trees, birds steal a glance,
Swaying like dancers in a clumsy trance.
A squirrel drops an acorn with flair,
And giggles echo in summer's warm air.

The petals laugh, swirling around,
While the wind spins tales, all silly and sound.
A lizard suns with audacious pride,
Winking at the world, it's harmlessly snide.

a Dreamscape

Clouds drift lazily, dressed in white sheets,
While ants debate the best way for treats.
A breeze joins in: 'Don't take life too fast!'
As even the grass tries a jig while it lasts.

Butterflies flaunt their vibrant new gear,
While bugs sing ballads that only they hear.
The skies chuckle softly, gold hues abound,
As dreams skip along in this wonderland found.

Marooned in Nature's Embrace

A cat naps soundly, avoiding the buzz,
While crickets compose a tune that still does.
A crow caws loudly, with laughter it mocks,
As shadows dance playfully on wooden blocks.

The monkeys swing by, stealing bananas, so bold,
While daisies shake heads, 'This life is pure gold!'
A turtle blinks slowly, pondering fate,
Wishing on stars that loners create.

The Gentle Embrace of Sunlit Fronds

Fronds wave hello to bees in their suits,
While sunbeams giggle, their golden roots.
A rabbit hops by, with style much too grand,
Chasing its tail through the warm, bouncy land.

The creatures conspire to throw a grand bash,
With fruit as confetti, a colorful splash.
But the sloth arrives late, with a leisurely grin,
"A party?" he mumbles, "Did I miss the best spin?"

Under the Canopy of Untold Stories

Whispers float softly of tales long gone,
As creatures convene with the rise of the dawn.
A wise old owl, with spectacles gleams,
Says, 'You can't trust squirrels; they plot with your dreams!'

While mushrooms debate if they can take flight,
Dancing in shadows, eyes brimming with light.
The breeze chuckles softly at life's sweet parade,
As laughter erupts in nature's charade.

Where Nature's Paintbrush Dances

Under leafy hats, we prance and play,
Sipping coconut drinks, we shout hooray!
The parrot squawks jokes, quite the funny chap,
While lizards do the cha-cha, creating a flap.

Sun-kissed cheeks glow, laughter fills the air,
A monkey swings by, with a mischievous flair.
He steals our snacks, oh what a cheeky tease,
As we chase him around, swatting at the bees.

Colorful blooms nod, in rhythm with glee,
They whisper sweet secrets, just for you and me.
Life's a comedy stage under this vibrant dome,
Where nature's palette paints a whimsical home.

Shadowed Corners of Tropical Bliss

In dim-bright corners, a turtle takes a nap,
While we spin tall tales, like a crazy chap.
The crabs join in, wearing shells as their hats,
As they dance in circles, defying all stats.

A breeze tickles cheeks, oh what a delight,
As birds start a choir, from morning till night.
The hammock swings low, a comfy cocoon,
We wave to the flora, dancing to the tune.

Pineapples gossip, high on their thrones,
While pesky ants march, making funny groans.
With laughter and snacks, the day fades away,
Under leafy umbrellas, we whimsically stay.

In the Heart of Green Serenity

Among leafy giants, we find our fun,
Tickling tall grasses, as we run and run.
A bee tries to waltz, but stumbles in flight,
It's a true spectacle, what a hilarious sight!

The frogs croak a tune, a low bass refrain,
As we join the chorus, embracing the rain.
The sloths call for help, but they move so slow,
We burst into giggles, watching them go.

A bright sun sets low, painting skies in jest,
In nature's embrace, we've found our zest.
With every new turn, more laughter we find,
In our green paradise, happiness entwined.

Rippling Lights and Gentle Breezes

Dancing like jellyfish, the shadows sway,
While we try to mimic, in a fun-filled way.
The breeze tells tales of far-off lands,
As we boast about our epic sunburned tans.

The sunset's a joker, painting skies bright,
As crickets start chirping, a band in the night.
Bouncing on waves, we share silly grins,
Counting all our wins, like accidental spins.

The stars wink down, enjoying the show,
While the moon laughs softly, putting on a glow.
In this magical space, with laughter and cheers,
We dance with the whispers, casting away fears.

Secrets of the Swaying Sanctuary

Beneath the leaves, a secret speaks,
A squirrel's dance in leafy peaks.
It twists and twirls, a comic show,
While I just sit, with snack in tow.

The breeze arrives, a gentle tease,
It rustles strands with carefree ease.
A coconut drops, what a surprise!
I dodge and laugh—oh, how time flies!

Sunbeams play hide and seek with me,
As shadows stretch beneath the tree.
A hammock swings, my latest scheme,
To nap and dream, or so I deem.

But then a bird sings out of tune,
I swear it's causing quite the swoon.
With giggles shared on this fine day,
The swaying leaves know how to play.

Lullabies of the Leafy Retreat

In leafy cradles, whispers hum,
As chubby squirrels begin to drum.
Each nut they toss, a clumsy feat,
I chuckle softly, can't help but greet.

The shadows shift, as sunlight fades,
A chameleon flips in leafy shades.
It tries to blend, but fails to hide,
I laugh aloud, no need for pride.

A breeze meanders, tofu thick,
A sly breeze wiggles, all too slick.
It tickles my nose, a playful muse,
I sneeze aloud—oh, what a ruse!

While lizard peers with sparkly eye,
I swear it winks, but I can't deny.
As day embarks, the sun bows low,
These lullabies help time to flow.

Tides of Calm in Fronded Nooks

The palms sway gently, they're quite the crew,
One whispers secrets—oh, how they grew!
I sit enthralled, popcorn in hand,
As nature's humor sweeps the land.

A lizard slides on slick terrain,
It trips and lands with no disdain.
With a flip of its tail, it takes a bow,
I can't help laughing—what a wow!

Clouds drift in like sleepy sheep,
I yawn and stretch, but I can't sleep.
The wind nudges me to dance along,
In this leafy nook, it feels so wrong!

Yet here I stay, in giggles and fits,
With palm fronds swaying, and nature's skits.
Each laugh a wave, a soothing balm,
This silly place, a tide of calm.

Love Letters to the Verdant Sky

The sky writes notes in fluffy white,
While birds collide in comic flight.
A parakeet stumbles, fluffs its plume,
I laugh aloud—what a colorful room!

The whispers float on gentle breeze,
As grasses gossip, setting hearts at ease.
The sun winks down, a playful star,
While ants parade in line—how bizarre!

With every twirl, the leaves extend,
A ticklish breeze, a quirky friend.
I pen my thoughts on crooked bark,
In this lush land, we leave our mark.

Each moment spent in nature's hush,
Brings hearty giggles; I feel the rush.
These letters fly, both near and far,
In this green world, we shine like stars.

Lost in the Green Embrace

Underneath the leafy crowns,
I lost my way, or was it found?
A squirrel snickered from a tree,
'This place is quite the labyrinth, see!'

With tangled roots beneath my feet,
I thought I saw a dancing beet.
But it was just my shadow's dance,
A clumsy fool in fate's own chance.

The lizards laughed, they had a ball,
As I tripped over a slippery wall.
With every step, I spun around,
In this green maze, joy I found.

Each palm held secrets, leaves of grace,
I twirled and laughed in this wide space.
Though lost in this emerald spree,
I felt quite at home, did I agree!

A Symphony of Shadows

Sunbeams poke through leafy hues,
Creating tunes, the wind renews.
A monkey's chatter, so divine,
I almost thought it could be mine!

A dance of shadows, loud and bright,
The palm trees giggle day and night.
They poke fun at my silly hat,
Swaying gently, what's with that?

A crow commented, wise old sage,
'You look like you've stepped off the page!'
I took a bow, a grand display,
As laughter echoed, hip-hip-hooray!

The leaves rustle with a cheeky cheer,
"Who needs sunshine when friends are near?"
With each chuckle, our spirits soared,
In this shadow realm, we were adored!

Sunlit Dreams in a Leafy Retreat

A hammock swung between two trees,
I took a nap, as light breezes tease.
Woke up to find my snack was gone,
The pesky birds had staged a con!

I laughed aloud in mock dismay,
'That was my cake, you feathered bray!'
A parrot chuckled, 'Want some pie?'
I thought, "A bird chef? Gimme a try!"

In leafy dreams, I chased a bee,
But it buzzed off, far too free.
The palms joined in with rustling glee,
"Don't worry mate, just wait and see!"

With every giggle from the green,
My sunlit dream turned quite obscene.
But in this laughter, so divine,
I found the best of summer's wine!

The Palm's Song at Dusk

As daylight ebbs, the palms begin,
A chorus forms, thick and thin.
Each leaf a note, swaying low,
They serenade the twilight glow.

"Hey there, human, have a seat!
Join our show, it'll be a treat!"
A breeze, a chuckle, whispers near,
"Relax yourself, dismiss that fear!"

I plopped right down, took in the scene,
With palms that danced, so soft and green.
A raccoon peeked from leafy shade,
"Life's a stage and look—parade!"

As stars emerged, the laughter swelled,
The palms proclaimed, "We're never quelled!"
In evening's light, we sang along,
In every sway, we found our song!

Oasis of Dappled Light

Beneath the fronds I lay my head,
A coconut drops; I dodge instead.
The lizards laugh, they pull a prank,
I toast the sun with my cold drink tank.

The breeze whispers jokes only I know,
As ants march by, putting on a show.
I try to nap, but the squawking bird,
Sings off-key, how absurd, absurd!

Sandy toes and a sunburned nose,
Sunbathing 'til a crab tail-doze.
I giggle at the waves' grand retreat,
They tickle my feet, oh, such a treat!

A hammock swings with a gentle sway,
My snack attacks, they start a buffet.
I munch and munch, but wait, what's that?
A seagull plots—a sudden spat!

Serenity Amidst Leafy Giants

Under great giants, I find my space,
The squirrels play tag, what a wild race!
A monkey swings in, brave and spry,
Stealing my snack, oh my, oh my!

The foliage whispers, secrets it keeps,
While I try hard not to fall asleep.
A toucan shouts, making a scene,
I swear he just called me a bean!

I stretch my limbs, feeling so free,
Taking bets on who'll climb the tree.
The shadows giggle, toss me a wink,
As I ponder if I could swim or sink.

An iguana joins with style so grand,
Decreeing that today is a sunbathing band.
I join the parade, life full of glee,
Who knew nature could be this zany?

Dancing Shadows Below the Crown

Shadows waltz, their feet never tire,
While I dance too, but on a wire!
Trips and slips, my clumsy display,
I bow to the palms, what can I say?

The ground below cracks jokes all day,
While I fumble and lose my way.
My drink spills out, a fruity mess,
The breeze just chuckles, oh what a stress!

A parrot squawks wisdom, oh so clever,
"Dance like the wind, let go, forever!"
My moves are odd, but I don't care,
Pineapple crown, I'm lost in flair.

The shadows join, we make quite a crew,
With flips and giggles, the day feels new.
Together we shuffle, misfit parade,
In this wild dream, I'm unafraid!

The Rustle of Tropical Dreams

Rustling leaves, a tickle of fate,
A breeze brings laughter, nothing's too great.
I throw my hands up, give it a try,
Then trip on my flip-flops, oh me, oh my!

The palms above cheer in a rustling chant,
While a crab does the cha-cha, quite gallant!
My lemonade's gone—did the squirrel sip?
It's a tropical party, come join the trip!

With each gentle sway, the world feels right,
On the dance floor of grass, through day and night.
While I sip my coconut, all eyes on me,
A turtle judges my rhythm with glee!

In dreams of sun and laughter I lay,
Surrounded by joy, come what may.
The rustle of joy, my heart it redeems,
In this quirky haven, I dance with my dreams!

Dance of Leaves in Stillness

The leaves do wiggle, twist, and sway,
Like hippos trying to dance ballet.
With branches flailing, all in jest,
They cheer for squirrels, put to the test.

The shadows play a game of tag,
While laughter echoes with a wag.
The sun peeks through with a cheeky grin,
As nature's party spins and spins.

The breeze brings tunes, a rustling song,
A chorus where critters all belong.
The air is thick with giggles galore,
In the grove where the giggling uproar.

A laughing branch lowers to pry,
As time does tick, the moments fly.
To dance with leaves, a funny affair,
In leafy dress, with nary a care.

A Haven from the Sun's Gaze

Oh, gather round, the light is hot,
We've found a space that's cool, quite a lot.
Where shadows stretch like lazy cats,
And pigeons strut like converts to hats.

Beneath our shelter, we sip our tea,
The ants march by, so carefree.
With every sip, we jest and mock,
While geckos pose like stars on a rock.

The sunburned fella next to me,
Wishes for shade and quite agrees.
"Is it the heat or just your charm?"
He pets the grass, it bends, but won't harm.

As sunbeams bounce, we laugh and tease,
The trees all chuckle in the breeze.
In this refuge, our giggles rise,
To tease the sun and its bright blue skies.

Secrets Held in Green Tresses

The leaves are whispering, what a chat,
About the squirrel who thinks he's a cat.
They giggle softly, secrets to share,
Of the raccoon's hat—a comical flair.

In tangled vines and emerald strands,
Tales of mischief pulled from their hands.
"Who stole the acorn?" they muse and laugh,
While the wind joins in, a breezy gaffe.

A chameleon hiding in plain sight,
Waves to a grasshopper, who jumps in fright.
The stories tumble like leaves in October,
As fruit flies dance like a disco rober.

So gather round, oh leafy crew,
For tales of haps that just won't do.
In tangled tresses, secrets unfurl,
In nature's humor, a wondrous swirl.

Beneath a Thousand Leafy Hearts

Underneath this leafy dome,
A raccoon declares, "I call this home!"
With shadows dripping, cool and wide,
He takes a nap; the world's his slide.

The birds throw shade, with cheeky chirps,
While ants march on, with little jerks.
Each twig a bench, each leaf a bed,
Frogs croak jokes, while we just tread.

In this haven, laughter's the sound,
Giggling gigabytes, all around.
As flowers bloom, we share our cheer,
With leaves above, there's naught to fear.

A breeze sweeps in, a tickling breeze,
As we swap stories, aim to please.
With a thousand hearts, we grow so bold,
In nature's grasp, just as foretold.

Tropical Breezes Weave Stories

The parrot squawks of gossip bright,
As crab and coconut share delight.
A monkey swings with playful flair,
While beach balls fly, and laughter fills the air.

Palm fronds wave like hands at play,
Inviting all to join the fray.
The sun peeks through in a winking jest,
As flip-flops race to find the best nest.

With each breeze that jostles the trees,
Tales of mishaps drift with ease.
A sunburned pig in shades so bright,
Chasing his tail – what a silly sight!

So gather round, my friends so dear,
With sandy toes and icy beer.
For in this land of jocular dreams,
Life's but a punchline, bursting at the seams.

Sunlight Danced with Shadows

Sunlight spun on the dancer's floor,
While shadows giggled behind the door.
A gecko slid, a flash of green,
With moves so slick, like he's a queen!

A crab in shades tried to look cool,
But tripped on sand like a silly fool.
The breeze cackled, it knew the score,
As sun-tans turned to burnt s'mores!

A skeptical turtle offered a frown,
"Why is everyone flopping 'round?"
With a slow-motion roll, quite absurd,
He claimed, "I've totally lost my word!"

Yet here and now, we dance with glee,
While dipsy doodles set us free.
In this sunlit kitchen of chaos divine,
Silly moments are perfectly fine!

The Enchanted Thicket

Once in a thicket not too far,
Where squirrels played with a fallen star.
They built a castle from scraps of dream,
And held a feast with wild ice cream!

A raccoon in a tuxedo gave a toast,
To the friends who loved to frolic the most.
With berries pulsing on plates so bright,
They danced with fireflies in the night.

A hedgehog fell into the punch,
And squeaked, "I guess this was my lunch!"
While owls hooted at silly sights,
In a moonlit gala of whimsical delights.

So join the jest in this leafy place,
Where every giggle shares the space.
With harmonies of laughter and cheer,
The thicket thrives—let's give a cheer!

Where the Earth Meets the Sky

Where horizons blend in comedy,
Laughter floats upon the sea.
A crab with dreams of Broadway fame,
Danced clumsily—it's all a game!

The sun and clouds share a witty debate,
Who's the brightest? Who's first-rate?
As waves clap their hands in sweet applause,
Beneath the trees, without a cause.

A dolphin zoomed, with a cheeky smile,
While a clam tried to think of a clever style.
In this theatre of nature's play,
Every character has something to say.

So lift your spirits, let's unite,
In this merry land where hearts take flight.
For underneath this vast blue affair,
We find the fun, in sunny air!

The Canopy's Embrace

Under leafy branches, we can chill,
Sipping coconut water, what a thrill!
A parrot squawks jokes, he's quite the show,
While squirrels plan mischief, plotting below.

A lizard sunbathes, like he owns the place,
Offers sunblock tips, with a scaly face.
While ants debate fashion, in shades of brown,
I just want a hammock, to lie upside down.

The breeze whispers secrets from high above,
A dance party breaking, amongst the love.
With each swinging frond, a new laugh ignites,
As shadows perform, under starry nights.

So here's to the laughter, and all things bright,
Under this big top, we revel in light.
Nature's comedy club, everyone's a hit,
In leafy embrace, there's no chance of a twit.

Cool Refuge from the Blaze

Heat sizzles around, like bacon gone wrong,
But under these palms, you can't help but sing a song.
The sun's a bold player, trying to bake,
While a mischievous breeze makes the palm fronds shake.

A crab strolls by, with a swaggering strut,
Challenging iguanas, but what a big gut!
Each splash from the sea, is a joke on repeat,
As we giggle at dolphins and their squirty sweet feat.

Flip-flops are flying, someone just fell,
They'll blame it on seaweed, it's a tropical spell.
Laughter erupts, like waves on the shore,
In this refuge from heat, we couldn't ask for more.

As the sun bows low, our giggles won't cease,
With laughter and drinks, our fun will increase.
In this cool retreat, where humor runs high,
We'll banter and bask 'neath the wide open sky.

Where Silt and Sand Converge

Where two worlds meet, oh what a sight,
With sand in my shorts, I'm feeling just right.
A crab builds a castle, one grain at a time,
While I trip on my towel, what's this, oh sublime!

Seagulls pretend to be experts of flight,
As I attempt yoga, managing with all my might.
Each pose turns to planks, I'm one with the earth,
While sand gives a tickle, enhancing my mirth.

Children are laughing, kites high in the air,
As parents all nap, without a single care.
We trade our tall tales of not-so-fun trips,
As waves play a melody, we serenade slips.

From sunburn to giggles, the stories are grand,
As shells join our laughter, washed up on the sand.
In this quirky junction, life feels like a game,
Where laughter and silliness truly became.

Mirage of a Tropical Dream

A tropical vision, serving up laughs,
As we search for coconuts, but find only halves.
The sun's a prankster, he's trying to tan,
While crabs make a poker game, what's their plan?

My drink just spilled, right into my lap,
A tropical splash, thanks to that naughty sap.
The breeze joins the fun, tickling my nose,
As the palm trees dance, in a comedic pose.

Waves clap along, as they crash with delight,
Fish joke around, in their underwater flight.
Turtles seem busy, hurrying no matter,
With shells like briefcases, they're late for their chatter.

As night falls gently, with stars up high,
We tell tales of blunders, mixed in with a sigh.
In this silly paradise, we find our gleam,
Living our best lives, in a humorous dream.

An Invitation to Tropical Calm

Come sip a drink, the sun won't bite,
Grab a coconut, feel the delight!
Laughter echoes, the breeze does tease,
Join the party, all worries freeze.

Bees are buzzing, they want some fun,
Dancing to rhythms, under the sun!
Swaying to tunes, with a twist and a shout,
In our paradise, there's no doubt.

Flip-flops flying, hats in the air,
Sunburned noses, with no care to spare!
Friends gather 'round, like ants to sweets,
In this wild land, life's pure treats.

So pack your bags and leave your shoes,
Let's trade the grind for dance and blues!
In this tropic haven, join our cheer,
Where every moment is filled with beer.

Gathering Light Under Fronded Archways

Under leafy canopies, we frolic and play,
With fresh mango juice and the sun's golden ray.
Chasing chickens, laughing loud,
In this wild jungle, we're part of the crowd.

The piñata swings, a burst of delight,
Candy rains down, oh what a sight!
The shy toucan watches the fray,
As we stumble and giggle our cares away.

Coconuts roll, oh what a mess!
Slippers flying, under duress!
Yet in the chaos, we find our groove,
At the fronded dance, we learn to move.

So come one, come all, with joy in your heart,
Let's create memories, let laughter start!
For under these leaves, we'll never feel blue,
Just a festive gathering, of me and of you.

Shade-Haven of the Blessed Light

In this blessed nook, where laughter spills,
The wind plays tricks with its playful thrills.
Shade does cradle silly little bees,
While we sip on breezes, and giggle with ease.

A sing-along croaks from somewhere near,
A frog chimes in, quite the weird career!
Bajo el sol, we sway and spin,
Life here is nutty, let the games begin!

Bamboo flutes sound a tantalizing song,
Tiny crabs march, they won't take long.
We'll dance like there's no tomorrow, my friend,
For in this haven, worries do end.

So gather around, let's toast the day,
In this light-filled space, we'll find our way.
With smiles as bright as the sun's sweet glow,
In this joyful retreat, together we'll flow.

Poetry Written in Leaf and Light

Leaves whisper tales under the sun,
Each word a giggle, each laugh is fun!
Let's draw silly faces on sandy shores,
With grains of rice and sticky s'mores.

A parrot squawks, causing a stir,
While tropic tunes invite us to purr.
With that sunburned bum, oh what a sight!
We dance like dervishes in the golden light.

In this memoir of laughter and play,
Come craft your dreams, let worries sway.
For when the moon peeks through the leaves,
We write our stories, as the night weaves.

So grab your sunhat and join the crew,
In this giddy glade, we'll rendezvous.
With every chuckle, life feels so right,
In this playful chaos, we shine so bright.

Dappled Dreams and Ocean Breezes

Beneath the green, where laughter flows,
Sunblock fails, now who knows?
Frogs play tunes on ukulele strings,
While loungers nap and seagull sings.

Flip-flops squeak on sandy trails,
Ice cream drips, well, it never fails.
The sun's a prankster, so bold and bright,
Sipping coconut, we feel just right.

A frisbee flies, but where it lands?
In grandma's lap or in the sands?
Giggles echo, promises made,
In this realm where time's delayed.

With waves that dance and flip around,
We've lost the ball, it can't be found!
A crab waves back, its own style of cheer,
Who knew a beach could bring such cheer?

Flickers of Light on Gentle Waves

Seashells whisper their ancient tales,
While sunscreen turns into jelly trails.
Napping dolphin steals my seat,
And leaves behind the salty treat.

Starfish plotting their daring escape,
Clams bragging with a silken drape.
Waves throw parties with salty cake,
If you get too close, make no mistake!

Gull swoops down, what a cheeky bird!
Steals my sandwich, not even stirred.
With tails that flick and fins that splish,
How is life a water dish?

A dance-off starts on splashing shores,
Even the crabs join in, of course!
As sunlight twinkles on fun-filled brine,
Here, the jokes and giggles entwine.

Where the Tropics Kiss the Sky

Luminous blooms rivaling the sun,
A toucan's gossip, isn't it fun?
Bananas giggle in tree-top clubs,
While iguanas bounce in leafy hubs.

The breeze is mischievous, dances about,
Twirling our hats with an effortless shout.
Papaya poofs like a clown with flair,
While mangoes tumble, unaware of their care.

Parrots chuckle with wise-crack tones,
Is that the sound of falling bones?
Nope, just coconuts dropping with cheer,
Please dodge those, or else shed a tear!

A sunburned nose and laughter that's bright,
Love in the air, oh what a sight!
In this space where palms play a tune,
Life hits a high, like a bongo's croon.

Below the Canopy, Time Stands Still

Violet pitch, where humor sways,
Raccoons debate on playful ways.
Monkeys swing with invisible tricks,
Dropping mangoes, oh what a mix!

Lianas hang like a nature's vine,
Creaky trees share their best line.
Breezes rustle, weaving mischief,
As time forgets its usual gift.

Chillin' deep, shade's embrace tight,
Caterpillars dance with all their might.
Laughter echoed from leaves so green,
Nature's stage, oh, what a scene!

Grasshoppers float, with a guitar sound,
In this theater, bliss unbound.
While above, the branches twist and curl,
In this leafy haven, we give it a whirl.

Rooted Moments in Tropical Glow

Underneath the tall trees, laughter springs,
Silly monkeys dance while the parrot sings.
Chasing shadows, we tumble and fall,
Giggles echo loudly, a joyful call.

The sun drips down like honey on toast,
We argue over who can swim the most.
With coconut hats and sand in our toes,
Time slips by like a soft summer rose.

An iguana judges our beachside splats,
While we build castles, look—here come the rats!
They dig and dig, it's a sight to see,
This beach is a circus, come laugh with me.

Under flickering lights as the day turns dim,
We dance by the sea, a rhythm, a whim.
With friends all around and smiles that won't fade,
These moments are treasures, sweet memories made.

Shades of Solitude in Paradise

Beneath the broad leaves, a nap turns to plans,
Dreaming of pizza and fresh coconut cans.
A squirrel steals snacks with a mischievous glare,
We wave our arms, but he doesn't care!

A hammock sways gently, caught in a breeze,
I ponder my life while I swat at the bees.
What's better than napping with dreams from a book?
Only a snack and more napping—that's the hook!

Friends come in, with laughter and pies,
They trip on my toes, oh, what a surprise!
We stumble and giggle, the sun's dipping low,
Shades of mischief and joy start to glow.

The stars start to twinkle, the moon's up above,
We snicker and shout, this place that we love.
With heart-shaped cookies and tales of the day,
In the shadows of laughter, forever we'll play.

Meadow of Dreams Beneath Leafy Skies

In the green expanse, where the daisies peek,
We plot our adventures, giggling unique.
A frog hops by, with a confident sound,
We cheer him on—oh, he's gravity-bound!

The ants hold a race, oh what a bizarre sight,
They scuttle and tumble, what a clumsy flight!
We cheer for the fast ones, but all are a blur,
The prize is a crumb—it's a grand ole spur!

Butterflies flutter, making grand speeches,
Over myself, my jam sandwich, it reaches!
With grass in our hair, and dirt on our hands,
We disappear, covered in nature's fine brands.

As the sun starts to dip, we shout in delight,
Chasing our shadows, it feels just right.
In dreams made of laughter, in meadows we dwell,
With friends that are silly, we're under their spell.

Tucked Away in Nature's Grasp

Hiding in bushes like kids on a quest,
We sneak and we giggle, we're doing our best.
A raccoon looks puzzled, what's with all the noise?
Did he find our treasure, or steal all our toys?

Swinging on vines like prancing young fools,
With mud on our knees, we invent new schools.
The rules of our game? It's all just a laugh,
Who cares if we land on a slippery calf?

Clouds float above, with faces that wink,
They giggle with us, oh, what do you think?
As raindrops come dancing, we shout and we play,
Forget the umbrella, let's splash through the day!

With night on the way, we find our sweet hide,
Tucked under blankets, our laughter can't bide.
In this cradle of whimsy, we breathe and we cheer,
These moments of joy, forever held near.

Tranquil Tides of Rustling Green

Under the leaves, a lizard grins,
Gazing at the world, where chaos spins.
A breeze tickles toes, a soft, sweet tease,
While ants march by, all dressed in keys.

Squirrels engage in a nutty debate,
Who stole whose snack? Oh, it's hard to sate!
Palm fronds wave like they're in a dance,
As we laugh out loud, lost in a trance.

A sleeping cat dreams of royal fame,
Chasing after shadows, oh what a game!
The sun dips low, time to plot a feast,
For laughter and joy, we are all increased.

So let's raise our cups to the antics here,
In a world lush and wild, oh, bring on the cheer!
With giggles and grins, we toast to the scene,
In this playful paradise, forever serene.

The Serenity of Hidden Groves

Beneath the fronds, the rabbits hop,
Playing tag among the greenery bop.
A squirrel with style, in a bow tie,
Sips from a coconut, oh my, oh my!

The sun peeks through, a cheeky spy,
While birds gossip loudly, flapping by.
"Did you hear about the turtle's race?
He took a nap! What a slow-paced chase!"

The air is fragrant, filled with sweet zest,
As monkeys swing in their fancy best.
Monkey see, monkey climb, joy in the air,
With giggles and grumbling of happy despair.

So here's to the laughter beneath leafy skies,
With nature's jesters, the wild ones, so wise.
In groves rich and green, where humor flows,
Life's comedic play unfolds, who really knows?

Tropical Reverie at Dusk

As daylight fades, the iguanas prance,
In their best attire, they hop, they dance.
Palms sway gently, no one seems to care,
The breeze whispers secrets, what a lovely affair.

Crickets begin their evening song,
While raccoons tag along, singing along.
A feast of fruits laid out on the ground,
"Who's raiding our picnic? Alert the hound!"

Frogs croak complaints from their lily pad seats,
While fish toss jokes in their watery beats.
With laughter and light, the stars twinkle bright,
In this tropical realm, all is just right.

So raise your drinks, let the tales unwind,
With humor and fun, our hearts intertwined.
In dusk's embrace, we dance and we jest,
Together in joy, simply feeling blessed.

Reflections on the Water's Edge

At the water's brink, where the lilies grow,
A family of ducks puts on quite the show.
Mom quacks directions, while ducklings parade,
All in a line, oh what a charade!

The fish tell jokes with bubbles and splashes,
While turtles in slow-mo, make funny dashes.
"Why did the crab not share his pie?
Because it was shellfish!" Oh my, oh my!

A frog leaps out, takes a tiny bow,
Wearing a crown made from a green leaf now.
The sun reflects as it starts to sink,
In this goofy world, we ponder and think.

So here's to the mirth, the splashes, and fun,
In nature's own circus, we all become one.
With laughter and joy, we'll cherish this pledge,
Together, forever, by the water's edge.

Oasis of Tranquility

Beneath the leafy green, a deal went down,
A lizard swapped a hat for a shiny crown.
The sun got jealous, forgot to glare,
While crickets rang a song, light as air.

A squirrel chased a shadow, lost his way,
While ants began their conga, without delay.
The watermelon's grin was hard to miss,
As it juggled seeds in a summer bliss.

Lounge chairs turned into pirate ships,
Floating 'round on dreams with funny quips.
The breeze told a joke, but nobody laughed,
Except for a coconut that split in half.

So if you need a break from the daily grind,
Join the fest where mischief's entwined.
Where nature plays tricks, and laughter's the deal,
In this sunny spot where joy's surreal.

The Gentle Fall of Time's Embrace

Ticks and tocks take a silly trip,
As you stroll with a sandwich and an ice cream dip.
Time rolled in like a donut on a spree,
No hurry here, it's just you and the bee.

The clock grew legs and danced a jig,
While hourglasses waved, feeling big.
Tickling the sun, they swayed left and right,
Making shadows laugh, what a fun sight!

Footraces with snails caused an uproar,
While wise old owls debated at the core.
A pineapple crowned the lazy breeze,
Flipping through pages of dreams with ease.

So strip off your worries, come join this spree,
Where moments melt like ice cream, don't you see?
In this gentle chaos of time's sweet chase,
Every tick-tock has a funny face.

Whispers Beneath Fronds

Listen close, the leaves exchange a grin,
While squirrels plot mischief on a whim.
A breeze carries giggles, soft and sly,
As shadows peek out, winking by.

Chickens formed a band, with clucks like drums,
While frogs started rapping, calls like hums.
The sun wore shades, looking mighty cool,
While ducks played checkers, breaking the rule.

A gopher told secrets to hollow logs,
About the day the cows danced with frogs.
Laughter echoed through the vibrant scene,
Where silliness reigns, calm yet keen.

So hush, and hear the whispers around,
Where the funny beats of nature abound.
In these playful moments, life feels grand,
Join in the fun, take a whimsical stand.

Secrets of the Swaying Canopy

High above, the leaves conspire and play,
Swapping stories of the cheery day.
A monkey swung by, full of delight,
With bananas in hand, what a funny sight!

Clouds dressed in pajamas floated so low,
Grumbling about a lost sock in tow.
While shadows shared tales of embarrassing falls,
Laundry hanging high, nobody calls.

The sun threw a party, warmth in the air,
Inviting all critters with feathers and hair.
Balloons made of petals bobbed on the breeze,
As laughter erupted from laughter-loving trees.

So join the antics in the rustling leaves,
Where the world reveals what a smile achieves.
There's magic in the whispers, secrets unfold,
In this silly oasis where life is gold.

Whispers Beneath the Fronds

Beneath the fronds, the secrets hide,
Squirrels gossip, cats take pride.
Lizards dance with such great flair,
While the crows play truth or dare.

With sunburned noses, we stand still,
Upturned palms catch wayside thrill.
A parrot squawks, it sounds like sass,
While I ponder my sunscreen class.

The breeze comes sneaking, what a prank,
It lifts my hat, oh how it swank!
The ground is laughing, funny sight,
As my flip-flop takes to flight.

So let us linger, laugh and share,
Under this leafy, vibrant air.
With every chuckle, life's a game,
Beneath the palms, we stake our claim.

Shadows Caressed by Breezes

In shadows cast, the antics bloom,
A gopher twirls, an unexpected zoom.
Grasshoppers boast of leaps so grand,
While my lemonade slips from my hand.

Coconuts thump, a playful fall,
We dodge and weave, mustn't stall.
The crickets chirp a bedtime song,
As we giggle, where we belong.

Picnic snacks disappear in a blink,
A seagull's theft, oh, how we think!
With laughter lighter than the breeze,
We dance around tall swaying trees.

So let's embrace this foolish spree,
With giggles echoing, wild and free.
In every rustle, a joke takes flight,
In the gentle shadows, all feels right.

Dappled Light and Gentle Sway

In dappled light, the laughter sways,
While mermaids sing of sunny days.
A crab in costume, dancing proud,
Takes center stage and draws a crowd.

A frog jumps high — a leaping bet,
Watch out for swamps and the sun set!
With ice cream drips and sticky hands,
We plot our take on beachy lands.

The breeze plays tricks, a tug of war,
As hats float off, we chase and roar.
The palms just giggle, gently sway,
In this goofy, sunny ballet.

So come, let's bask in joy and cheer,
With every laugh, we conquer fear.
Among the greens, life's laughter grows,
Where joy and silliness freely flows.

Serenity Among the Treetops

At treetops high, the jokes unfold,
In branches, whispered tales retold.
A sloth pretends it's running late,
While a parakeet steals its fate.

A picnic planned, what a delight,
Till raccoons crash and start a fight.
With fruit gone missing, who's to say?
It's just a snack thief's funny play.

The sun peeks through with cheeky grins,
As fireflies twirl and spin their wins.
Each moment shared beneath the sky,
Turns ordinary days to a joyous high.

So let's enjoy these jests that bloom,
With shadows dancing, dispelling gloom.
Amongst the tops, where laughter thrives,
In this sweet spot, humor survives.

www.ingramcontent.com/pod-product-compliance
Lightning Source LLC
Chambersburg PA
CBHW072119070526
44585CB00016B/1500